BEST-LOVED
YEATS

BEST-LOVED
YEATS

selected by

MAIRÉAD ASHE FITZGERALD

THE O'BRIEN PRESS
DUBLIN

First published 2010 by The O'Brien Press Ltd.
12 Terenure Road East, Rathgar, Dublin 6, Ireland.
Tel: +353 1 4923333; Fax: +353 1 4922777
E-mail: books@obrien.ie; Website: www.obrien.ie

ISBN: 978-1-84717-148-1

1 2 3 4 5 6 7 8 9 10
10 11 12 13 14
Cover illustration: Emma Byrne
Editing, typesetting, layout and design:
The O'Brien Press Ltd
Printed in China by Kwong Fat Offset Printing Co Ltd.

The paper in this book is produced using pulp from managed forests.

Mairéad Ashe FitzGerald has contributed to many publications and is the
author of *Thomas Johnson Westropp (1860-1922) An Irish Antiquary* and *Exploring the
World of Colmcille*.

LIST OF ILLUSTRATIONS

TABLE OF CONTENTS

The Enchanted Land

The Romantic Idealist

Coole Park and Thoor Ballylee

War and Politics

Old Age and Death

WILLIAM BUTLER YEATS
THE POET AND IRELAND

illiam Butler Yeats was born in 1865, the son of John Butler Yeats, an artist whose forebears were Protestant churchmen in Sligo, and Susan Pollexfen who belonged to a Sligo merchant family. The Yeats family was to make a unique contribution to the cultural and artistic life of twentieth century Ireland: William Butler Yeats became the greatest poet writing in English in the twentieth century; his brother, Jack Yeats was one of the most gifted Irish painters of modern times; his sisters, Elizabeth and Susan, devoted their lives to artistic endeavours and were the founders of The Cuala Press.

THE ENCHANTED LAND

William Butler Yeats's relationship with his native county was one of the main influences in shaping his future as a great poet. For the young emerging poet, Sligo was a place of enchantment. While his artist father, adored by his son, but mercurial and unreliable, moved his family between Sligo, Dublin and London, long summers were spent in Sligo, and it was Sligo that fired William's poetic imagination.

He filled his mind with the lore of the people of the Sligo countryside, people who had within them, as he wrote, 'the vast and vague extravagance that lies at the bottom of the Celtic heart'.

He filled notebooks with the stories and folklore he heard from people such as Mary Battle, a local woman who had a fund of ancient lore. The old Celtic romances, stories of the Sídhe, the fairy hosts, the great heroes of the myths of the Celts, CuChulainn, Caoilte and Oisín, along with the fair Niamh were to inspire his poetry. Yeats's work, in turn, inspired and influenced others during the Irish Literary Revival.

The Otherworld, the land of eternal youth

'where beauty has no ebb, decay no flood,
But joy is wisdom, Time an endless song'

was part of everyday life to the people amongst whom Yeats spent his days as a boy. The countryside around Sligo was the gateway to that magical Otherworld; its placenames, Knocknarea, Ben Bulben, Glencar; Innishfree, the little island in Lough Gill and the woods around it, were to be immortalised in his poetry throughout his life, so that, together, they make for a part of Ireland which came to be known as 'The Yeats Country'.

Yeats's passion for the Celtic past provided him with a way of seeking answers to life's endless quest for the mystical. That same quest was to lead him to explore the occult in the 1890s and to membership of the Hermetic Order of The Golden Dawn.

His friendship with the old Fenian, John O'Leary, led Yeats into nationalism and he promoted the idea of a distinctive literature so that Irish people would realise their spiritual and cultural heritage.

THE ROMANTIC IDEALIST

In 1889 Yeats, at the age of twenty-three, met Maud Gonne in London, and with that meeting, as he wrote, 'the troubling of my life began'. He endured a tortured and hopeless love for her for over thirty years, during which time she was his muse, his inspiration, the embodiment of Ireland itself in his work. Gonne, unconventional, beautiful and independently wealthy, was the daughter of a British

Army major based at the Curragh, County Kildare. Dedicated to the cause of independence for Ireland, she threw herself into political activity. Yeats proposed marriage to her in 1891 without success and was to do so many times over the years. Unknown to Yeats, Gonne had a daughter, Iseult, in 1894, by her French lover, Lucien Millevoye. He was shocked and grieved when she married Major John MacBride in 1903. The couple separated in 1905 and Gonne was widowed in 1916 when MacBride was amongst the executed leaders after the Easter Rising. Yeats proposed marriage to her again, and on being refused, he proposed to her daughter, Iseult, who likewise declined his proposal.

The love poems he wrote to Maud Gonne are haunting, filled with symbolism, longing and sadness.

COOLE PARK AND THOOR BALLYLEE

Yeats's meeting with Augusta Lady Gregory in 1896 was another momentous turning point in his life. Born into an ascendancy family near Gort, through her marriage she became mistress of Coole Park estate in County Galway.

Like the much younger Yeats, Lady Gregory had

immersed herself in the lore and culture of the locality, Kiltartan, where Coole Park lay. Though belonging to the landowning class, her life was dedicated to furthering the literary revival in Ireland. Her home was a centre for writers of the day, and it was at Coole that the idea of a National Theatre was developed. The estate, with its Seven Woods, the great house and its lake, was to be immortalised in Yeats's work and provided him with an inspirational environment over many years. Recognising Yeats's genius, Lady Gregory gave him the stability and encouragement that he needed and was his friend and supporter until her death in 1932.

In 1917, Yeats bought Thoor Ballylee, a ruined medieval tower-house close to Coole Park. In the same year, he married a young Englishwoman, George Hyde-Lees, who was twenty-five years his junior. A scholarly and resourceful woman who recognized the genius in the man she married, she applied herself to managing his life and restoring Thoor Ballylee. Like Yeats, she was interested in the occult, and in this phase of his life, assisted by his wife, Yeats discovered automatic writing, a mediumistic script that provided material for poems that convey his ideas on the nature of historical change and decay. The medieval tower itself provided the setting for many of his poems and took on a powerful symbolism in his work.

YEATS, THE PUBLIC MAN

Yeats was a man of action too, devoted as he was to furthering Irish culture, founding the National Theatre, putting on plays, managing the Abbey Theatre and steering it through the early years. Always in the thick of things, he was outspoken both in his poetry and in public against what he perceived as the philistinism of the day. He forced Ireland to look at herself as a society. He famously harangued the audience that rioted on the opening night of Synge's *The Playboy of the Western World*. The rejection of the gift of Hugh Lane's fine collection of French Impressionist paintings by Dublin Corporation called forth his anger and he was to put much time and effort, along with Lady Gregory, Hugh Lane's aunt, into trying to retrieve them from the National Gallery in London when they were the subject of Lane's disputed Will.

Despite his ambiguous feelings about violent insurrection, Yeats found beauty in the events of Easter 1916, and his poems that were inspired by those events contributed to the aura of momentous history surrounding the Easter Rising. As a senator in the new Irish Free State, he contributed to the debates on the controversial subjects of divorce and the censorship of books.

Yeats was awarded the Nobel Prize for Literature in 1923, which he accepted as a representative of Irish literature and as an honour for his country, 'Europe's welcome to the Free State'.

OLD AGE AND DEATH

Yeats suffered from ill-health from the late 1920s, and in 1928 he left the Senate. From then onwards he took to wintering in the South of France for the sake of his health. But despite serious illness, Yeats, great artist that he was, continued to write poetry of true power and vigour. The eternal questions of old age and death preoccupied him and inspired some of his most profound work. Fearing the loss of creativity along with the passing of youth, he underwent a Steinach operation, reputed to provide a 'surgical reactivation' of the male, and had affairs with younger women.

'An aged man is but a paltry thing,
A tattered coat upon a stick,'

he writes in one of his greatest poems 'Sailing to Byzantium' which he included in his magisterial collection *The Tower* (1928).

William Butler Yeats left Ireland for the last time in October 1938 and died in Roquebrune in France on

28 January 1939. In 1938 his body was interred in Drumcliffe Churchyard, Sligo.

Anyone reading the works of William Butler Yeats will surely come to know and learn something about Ireland. His own wish, expressed in *The Celtic Twilight* (1893) was 'to show in a vision something of the face of Ireland to any of my own people who would look where I bid them'.

Mairéad Ashe FitzGerald
January 2010

THE ENCHANTED LAND

The Stolen Child

Where dips the rocky highland
Of Sleuth Wood in the lake,
There lies a leafy island
Where flapping herons wake
The drowsy water-rats;
There we've hid our faery vats,
Full of berries
And of reddest stolen cherries.
Come away, O human child!
To the waters and the wild
With a faery, hand in hand,
For the world's more full of weeping than you can understand.

Where the wave of moonlight glosses
The dim grey sands with light,
Far off by furthest Rosses
We foot it all the night,
Weaving olden dances,
Mingling hands and mingling glances
Till the moon has taken flight;
To and fro we leap
And chase the frothy bubbles,
While the world is full of troubles
And is anxious in its sleep.
Come away, O human child!
To the waters and the wild
With a faery hand in hand,
For the world's more full of weeping than you can understand.

Where the wandering water gushes
From the hills above Glen-Car,
In pools among the rushes
That scarce could bathe a star,
We seek for slumbering trout
And whispering in their ears
Give them unquiet dreams;
Leaning softly out
From ferns that drop their tears
Over the young streams.
Come away, O human child!
To the waters and the wild
With a faery, hand in hand,
For the world's more full of weeping than you can understand

Away with us he's going,
The solemn-eyed:
He'll hear no more the lowing
Of the calves on the warm hillside
Or the kettle on the hob
Sing peace into his breast,
Or see the brown mice bob
Round and round the oatmeal-chest.
For he comes, the human child,
To the waters and the wild
With a faery, hand in hand,
From a world more full of weeping than he can understand.

The places mentioned in 'The Stolen Child' were known to be the haunt of
fairies (Sídhe in the Irish) who were wont to carry off the souls of mortals
while they slept.

A Faery Song

Sung by the people of Faery over Diarmuid and Grania,
in their bridal sleep under a Cromlech

We who are old, old and gay,
O so old!
Thousands of years, thousands of years,
It all were told:

Give to these children, new from the world,
Silence and love;
And the long dew-dropping hours of the night,
And the stars above:

Give to these children, new from the world,
Rest far from men.
Is anything better, anything better?
Tell us it then:

Us who are old, old and gay,
O so old!
Thousands of years, thousands of years,
If all were told.

EXTRACT FROM

The Land of Heart's Desire

A VOICE [close to the door]

The wind blows out of the gates of the day,
The wind blows over the lonely of heart,
And the lonely of heart is withered away,
While the faeries dance in a place apart,
Shaking their milk-white feet in a ring,
Tossing their milk-white arms in the air:
For they hear the wind laugh, and murmur and sing
Of a land where even the old are fair,
And even the wise are merry of tongue;
But I heard a reed of Coolaney say,
'When the wind has laughed and murmured and sung,
'The lonely of heart is withered away!'

These lines come from Yeats's verse drama The Land of Heart's
Desire *in which a young bride is enticed away to fairyland
by the Sídhe on May Eve.*

The Hosting of the Sidhe

The host is riding from Knocknarea
And over the grave of Clooth-na-Bare;
Caoilte tossing his burning hair,
And Niamh calling Away, come away:
Empty your heart of its mortal dream.
The winds awaken, the leaves whirl round,
Our cheeks are pale, our hair is unbound,
Our breasts are heaving, our eyes are agleam,
Our arms are waving, our lips are apart;
And if any gaze on our rushing band,
We come between him and the deed of his hand,
We come between him and the hope of his heart.
The host is rushing 'twixt night and day,
And where is there hope or deed as fair?
Caoilte tossing his burning hair,
And Niamh calling Away, come away.

*The Slua Sídhe or the fairy host were believed to travel in the whirling
wind as it swept through the countryside. Niamh was the fairy princess who
enticed Oisín of the Fianna to spend three hundred years in Tír na nÓg, the
Otherworld.*

The Song of Wandering Aengus

I went out to the hazel wood,
Because a fire was in my head,
And cut and peeled a hazel wand,
And hooked a berry to a thread;
And when white moths were on the wing,
And moth-like stars were flickering out,
I dropped the berry in a stream
And caught a little silver trout.

When I had laid it on the floor
I went to blow the fire aflame,
But something rustled on the floor,
And some one called me by my name:
It had become a glimmering girl
With apple blossom in her hair
Who called me by my name and ran
And faded through the brightening air.

Though I am old with wandering
Through hollow lands and hilly lands,
I will find out where she has gone,
And kiss her lips and take her hands;
And walk among long dappled grass,
And pluck till time and times are done
The silver apples of the moon,
The golden apples of the sun.

*Aengus was the mythical God of Love who resided at Brú na Bóinne
or Newgrange.*

The Lake Isle of Innisfree

I will arise and go now, and go to Innisfree,
And a small cabin build there, of clay and wattles made:
Nine bean-rows will I have there, a hive for the honey-bee,
And live alone in the bee-loud glade.

And I shall have some peace there, for peace comes dropping slow
Dropping from the veils of the morning to where the cricket
sings;
There midnight's all a glimmer, and noon a purple glow,
And evening full of the linnet's wings.

I will arise and go now, for always night and day
I hear lake water lapping with low sounds by the shore;
While I stand on the roadway, or on the pavements grey,
I hear it in the deep heart's core.

Yeats wrote this, probably his best known poem, in London.
He relates in his Autobiographies *how, on hearing the tinkle of water*
in a fountain in a shop window in Fleet Street, he was overcome
by homesickness for Sligo and by his longing for the solitude
of the Isle of Innishfree which lies close to the shore in Lough Gill.

The Fiddler of Dooney

When I play on my fiddle in Dooney,
Folk dance like a wave of the sea;
My cousin is priest in Kilvarnet,
My brother in Mocharabuiee.

I passed my brother and cousin:
They read in their books of prayer;
I read in my book of songs
I bought at the Sligo fair.

When we come at the end of time
To Peter sitting in state,
He will smile on the three old spirits,
But call me first through the gate;

For the good are always the merry,
Save by an evil chance,
And the merry love the fiddle,
And the merry love to dance:

And when the folk there spy me,
They will all come up to me,
With 'Here is the fiddler of Dooney!'
And dance like a wave of the sea.

Red Hanrahan's Song about Ireland

The old brown thorn-trees break in two high over Cummen Strand
Under a bitter black wind that blows from the left hand;
Our courage breaks like an old tree in a black wind and dies,
But we have hidden in our hearts the flame out of the eyes
Of Cathleen, the daughter of Houlihan.

The wind has bundled up the clouds high over Knocknarea,
And thrown the thunder on the stones for all that Maeve can say.
Angers that are like noisy clouds have set out hearts abeat;
But we have all bent low and low and kissed the quiet feet
Of Cathleen, the daughter of Houlihan.

The yellow pool has overflowed high up on Clooth-na-Bare,
For the wet winds are blowing out of the clinging air;
Like heavy flooded waters our bodies and our blood;
But purer than a tall candle before the Holy Rood
Is Cathleen, the daughter of Houlihan.

*Hanrahan was a poetic character invented by Yeats and was
probably based on the eighteenth century Munster poet
Eoghan Rua Ó Súilleabháin*

THE ROMANTIC
IDEALIST

He wishes for the Cloths of Heaven

Had I the heavens' embroidered cloths,
Enwrought with golden and silver light,
The blue and the dim and the dark cloths
Of night and light and the half-light,
I would spread the cloths under your feet:
But I, being poor, have only my dreams;
I have spread my dreams under your feet;
Tread softly because you tread on my dreams.

The Pity of Love

A pity beyond all telling
Is hid in the heart of love:
The folk who are buying and selling,
The clouds on their journey above,
The cold wet winds ever blowing,
And the shadowy hazel grove
Where mouse-grey waters are flowing,
Threaten the head that I love.

The Sorrow of Love

The brawling of a sparrow in the eaves,
The brilliant moon and all the milky sky,
And all that famous harmony of leaves,
Had blotted out man's image and his cry.

A girl arose that had red mournful lips
And seemed the greatness of the world in tears,
Doomed like Odysseus and the labouring ships
And proud as Priam murdered with his peers;

Arose, and on the instant clamorous eaves,
A climbing moon upon an empty sky,
And all that lamentation of the leaves,
Could but compose man's image and his cry.

The White Birds

I would that we were, my beloved, white birds on the foam of the sea!
We tire of the flame of the meteor, before it can fade and flee;
And the flame of the blue star of twilight, hung low on the rim of the sky,
Has awaked in our hearts, my beloved, a sadness that may not die.

A weariness comes from those dreamers, dew-dabbled, the lily and rose;
Ah, dream not of them, my beloved, the flame of the meteor that goes,
Or the flame of the blue star that lingers hung low in the fall of the dew:
For I would we were changed to white birds on the wandering foam: I and you!

I am haunted by numberless islands, and many a Danaan shore,
Where Time would surely forget us, and Sorrow come near us no more;
Soon far from the rose and the lily and fret of the flames would we be,
Were we only white birds, my beloved, buoyed out on the foam of the sea!

While walking on the cliffs at Howth one day, Maud Gonne told Yeats that if she had a choice
of being a bird, she would like to be a sea-gull above all.

Down by the Salley Gardens

Down by the salley gardens my love and I did meet;
She passed the salley gardens with little snow-white feet.
She bid me take love easy, as the leaves grow on the tree;
But I, being young and foolish, with her would not agree.

In a field by the river my love and I did stand,
And on my leaning shoulder she laid her snow-white hand.
She bid me take life easy, as the grass grows on the weirs;
But I was young and foolish, and now am full of tears.

*'Salley' or 'Sally' is the variety of willow which grows in hedgerows
and watery places. The poem is believed by some to have
been based on an old ballad which Yeats heard in Ballisodare, Sligo.*

The Ragged Wood

O hurry where by water among the trees
The delicate-stepping stag and his lady sigh,
When they have but looked upon their images —
Would none had ever loved but you and I!

Or have you heard that sliding silver-shoed
Pale silver-proud queen-woman of the sky,
When the sun looked out of his golden hood? —
O that none ever loved but you and I!

O hurry to the ragged wood, for there
I will drive all those lovers out and cry —
O my share of the world, O yellow hair!
No one has ever loved but you and I.

When You are Old

When you are old and grey and full of sleep,
And nodding by the fire, take down this book,
And slowly read, and dream of the soft look
Your eyes had once, and of their shadows deep;

How many loved your moments of glad grace,
And loved your beauty with love false or true,
But one man loved the pilgrim soul in you,
And loved the sorrows of your changing face;

And bending down beside the glowing bars,
Murmur, a little sadly, how Love fled
And paced upon the mountains overhead
And hid his face amid a crowd of stars.

No Second Troy

Why should I blame her that she filled my days
With misery, or that she would of late
Have taught to ignorant men most violent ways,
Or hurled the little streets upon the great,
Had they but courage equal to desire?
What could have made her peaceful with a mind
That nobleness made simple as a fire,
With beauty like a tightened bow, a kind
That is not natural in an age like this,
Being high and solitary and most stern?
Why, what could she have done, being what she is?
Was there another Troy for her to burn?

The Lover pleads with his Friend for Old Friends

Though you are in your shining days,
Voices among the crowd
And new friends busy with your praise,
Be not unkind or proud,
But think about old friends the most:
Time's bitter flood will rise,
Your beauty perish and be lost
For all eyes but these eyes.

The Folly of Being Comforted

One that is ever kind said yesterday:
'Your well-beloved's hair has threads of grey,
And little shadows come about her eyes;
Time can but make it easier to be wise
Though now it seems impossible, and so
All that you need is patience.'

                            Heart cries, 'No,
I have not a crumb of comfort, not a grain,
Time can but make her beauty over again:
Because of that great nobleness of hers
The fire that stirs about her, when she stirs,
Burns but more clearly. O she had not these ways
When all the wild summer was in her gaze.'

O heart! O heart! If she'd but turn her head,
You'd know the folly of being comforted.

Never Give all the Heart

Never give all the heart, for love
Will hardly seem worth thinking of
To passionate women if it seem
Certain, and they never dream
That it fades out from kiss to kiss;
For everything that's lovely is
But a brief, dreamy, kind delight.
O never give the heart outright.
For they, for all smooth lips can say,
Have given their hearts up to the play.
And who would play it well enough
If deaf and dumb and blind with love?
He that made this knows all the cost,
For he gave all his heart and lost.

The Old Men Admiring Themselves in the Water

I heard the old, old men say,
'Everything alters,
And one by one we drop away.'
They had hands like claws, and their knees
Were twisted like the old thorn-trees
By the waters.
I heard the old, old men say,
'All that's beautiful drifts away
Like the waters.'

O Do Not Love Too Long

Sweetheart, do not love too long:
I loved long and long,
And grew to be out of fashion
Like an old song.

All through the years of our youth
Neither could have known
Their own thought from the other's,
We were so much at one.

I

To a Child Dancing in the Wind

Dance there upon the shore;
What need have you to care
For wind or water's roar?
And tumble out your hair
That the salt drops have wet;
Being young you have not known
The fool's triumph, nor yet
Love lost as soon as won,
Nor the best labourer dead
And all the sheaves to bind.
What need have you to dread
The monstrous crying of wind?

The child who is the subject of this poem and
'Two Years Later' was Iseult Gonne (1894–1954),
Maud Gonne's daughter by Lucien Millevoye.

Two Years Later

Has no one said those daring
Kind eyes should be more learn'd?
Or warned you how despairing
The moths are when they are burned?
I could have warned you; but you are young,
So we speak a different tongue.

O you will take whatever's offered
And dream that all the world's a friend,
Suffer as your mother suffered,
Be as broken in the end.
But I am old and you are young,
And I speak a barbarous tongue.

Memory

One had a lovely face,
And two or three had charm,
But charm and face were in vain
Because the mountain grass
Cannot but keep the form
Where the mountain hare has lain.

COOLE PARK AND THOOR BALLYLEE

The Wild Swans at Coole

The trees are in their autumn beauty,
The woodland paths are dry,
Under the October twilight the water
Mirrors a still sky;
Upon the brimming water among the stones
Are nine-and-fifty swans.

The nineteenth autumn has come upon me
Since I first made my count;
I saw, before I had well finished,
All suddenly mount
And scatter wheeling in great broken rings
Upon their clamorous wings.

I have looked upon those brilliant creatures,
And now my heart is sore.
All's changed since I, hearing at twilight,
The first time on this shore,
The bell-beat of their wings above my head,
Trod with a lighter tread.

Unwearied still, lover by lover,
They paddle in the cold
Companionable streams or climb the air;
Their hearts have not grown old;
Passion or conquest, wander where they will,
Attend upon them still.

But now they drift on the still water,
Mysterious, beautiful;
Among what rushes will they build,
By what lake's edge or pool
Delight men's eyes when I awake some day
To find they have flown away?

Written in a mood of intense depression in 1918 when
Yeats recognised the death of his love for Maud Gonne.

In the Seven Woods

I have heard the pigeons of the Seven Woods
Make their faint thunder, and the garden bees
Hum in the lime-tree flowers; and put away
The unavailing outcries and the old bitterness
That empty the heart. I have forgot awhile
Tara uprooted, and new commonness
Upon the throne and crying about the streets
And hanging its paper flowers from post to post,
Because it is alone of all things happy.
I am contented, for I know that Quiet
Wanders laughing and eating her wild heart
Among pigeons and bees, while that Great Archer,
Who but awaits His hour to shoot, still hangs
A cloudy quiver over Pairc-na-lee.

August 1902

My House

An ancient bridge, and a more ancient tower,
A farmhouse that is sheltered by its wall,
An acre of stony ground,
Where the symbolic rose can break in flower,
Old ragged elms, old thorns innumerable,
The sound of the rain or sound
Of every wind that blows;
The stilted water-hen
Crossing stream again
Scared by the splashing of a dozen cows;

A winding stair, a chamber arched with stone,
A grey stone fireplace with an open hearth,
A candle and written page.
Il Penseroso's Platonist toiled on
In some like chamber, shadowing forth
How the daemonic rage
Imagined everything.
Benighted travellers
From markets and from fairs
Have seen his midnight candle glimmering.

Two men have founded here. A man-at-arms
Gathered a score of horse and spent his days
In this tumultuous spot,
Where through long wars and sudden night alarms
His dwindling score and he seemed castaways
Forgetting and forgot;
And I, that after me
My bodily heirs may find,
To exalt a lonely mind,
Befitting emblems of adversity.

This poem, an extract from his long poetic work,
Meditations in Time of Civil War, *is about Thoor Ballylee,*
where Yeats and his young family spent much
of the period of the Irish Civil War (1922-1923).

A Prayer on going into my House

God grant a blessing on this tower and cottage
And on my heirs, if all remain unspoiled,
No table or chair or stool not simple enough
For shepherd lads in Galilee; and grant
That I myself for portions of the year
May handle nothing and set eyes on nothing
But what the great and passionate have used
Throughout so many varying centuries
We take it for the norm; yet should I dream
Sinbad the sailor's brought a painted chest,
Or image, from beyond the Loadstone Mountain,
That dream is a norm; and should some limb of the Devil
Destroy the view by cutting down an ash
That shades the road, or setting up a cottage
Planned in a government office, shorten his life,
Manacle his soul upon the Red Sea bottom.

A Cradle Song

The angels are stooping
Above your bed;
They weary of trooping
With the whimpering dead.

God's laughing in Heaven
To see you so good;
The Sailing Seven
Are gay with His mood.

I sigh that kiss you,
For I must own
That I shall miss you
When you have grown.

A Prayer for my Daughter

Once more the storm is howling, and half hid
Under this cradle-hood and coverlid
My child sleeps on. There is no obstacle
But Gregory's wood and one bare hill
Whereby the haystack- and roof-levelling wind,
Bred on the Atlantic, can be stayed;
And for an hour I have walked and prayed
Because of the great gloom that is in my mind.

I have walked and prayed for this young child an hour
And heard the sea-wind scream upon the tower,
And under the arches of the bridge, and scream
In the elms above the flooded stream;
Imagining in excited reverie
That the future years had come,
Dancing to a frenzied drum,
Out of the murderous innocence of the sea.

May she be granted beauty and yet not
Beauty to make a stranger's eye distraught,
Or hers before a looking-glass, for such,
Being made beautiful overmuch,
Consider beauty a sufficient end,
Lose natural kindness and maybe
The heart-revealing intimacy
That chooses right, and never find a friend.

Helen being chosen found life flat and dull
And later had much trouble from a fool,
While that great Queen, that rose out of the spray,
Being fatherless could have her way
Yet chose a bandy-leggèd smith for man.
It's certain that fine women eat
A crazy salad with their meat
Whereby the Horn of Plenty is undone.

In courtesy I'd have her chiefly learned;
Hearts are not had as a gift but hearts are earned
By those that are not entirely beautiful;
Yet many, that have played the fool
For beauty's very self, has charm made wise,
And many a poor man that has roved,
Loved and thought himself beloved,
From a glad kindness cannot take his eyes.

May she become a flourishing hidden tree
That all her thoughts may like the linnet be,
And have no business but dispensing round
Their magnanimities of sound,
Nor but in merriment begin a chase,
Nor but in merriment a quarrel.
O may she live like some green laurel
Rooted in one dear perpetual place.

My mind, because the minds that I have loved,
The sort of beauty that I have approved,
Prosper but little, has dried up of late,
Yet knows that to be choked with hate
May well be of all evil chances chief.
If there's no hatred in a mind
Assault and battery of the wind
Can never tear the linnet from the leaf.

An intellectual hatred is the worst,
So let her think opinions are accursed.
Have I not seen the loveliest woman born
Out of the mouth of Plenty's horn,
Because of her opinionated mind
Barter that horn and every good
By quiet natures understood
For an old bellows full of angry wind?

Considering that, all hatred driven hence,
The soul recovers radical innocence
And learns at last that it is self-delighting,
Self-appeasing, self-affrighting,
And that its own sweet will is Heaven's will;
She can, though every face should scowl
And every windy quarter howl
Or every bellows burst, be happy still.

And may her bridegroom bring her to a house
Where all's accustomed, ceremonious;
For arrogance and hatred are the wares
Peddled in the thoroughfares.
How but in custom and in ceremony
Are innocence and beauty born?
Ceremony's a name for the rich horn,
And custom for the spreading laurel tree.

June 1919

The poet's daughter, Anne Butler Yeats, was born
in February 1919.

To be Carved on a Stone at Thoor Ballylee

I, the poet William Yeats,
With old mill boards and sea-green slates,
And smithy work from the Gort forge,
Restored this tower for my wife George;
And may these characters remain
When all is ruin once again.

WAR
AND
POLITICS

September 1913

What need you, being come to sense,
But fumble in a greasy till
And add the halfpence to the pence
And prayer to shivering prayer, until
You have dried the marrow from the bone?
For men were born to pray and save:
Romantic Ireland's dead and gone,
It's with O'Leary in the grave.

Yet they were of a different kind,
The names that stilled your childish play,
They have gone about the world like wind,
But little time had they to pray
For whom the hangman's rope was spun,
And what, God help us, could they save?
Romantic Ireland's dead and gone,
It's with O'Leary in the grave.

Was it for this the wild geese spread
The grey wing upon every tide;
For this that all that blood was shed,
For this Edward Fitzgerald died,
And Robert Emmet and Wolfe Tone,
All that delirium of the brave?
Romantic Ireland's dead and gone,
It's with O'Leary in the grave.

Yet could we turn the years again,
And call those exiles as they were
In all their loneliness and pain,
You'd cry, 'Some woman's yellow hair
Has maddened every mother's son':
They weighed so lightly what they gave.
But let them be, they're dead and gone,
They're with O'Leary in the grave.

*Yeats deplores the loss of an earlier Irish nationalism which was
represented by idealists of the past. John O'Leary (1830-1907) of the
Fenian movement befriended the young Yeats, on whom he had a powerful
influence. The 'wild geese' were the Irishmen who left Ireland after 1691
when the Penal Laws were passed, preventing them from holding army
commissions. They fought in the armies of Europe, mainly in France,
Austria and Spain. Lord Edward FitzGerald (1763-98), an Irish MP
who joined the United Irishmen, was arrested during the Rising of 1798
and died of his wounds. Robert Emmet (1778-1803) led a failed
rebellion in 1803. He was betrayed, caught and hanged in Thomas Street,
Dublin. Theobald Wolfe Tone (1763-98) founded the United Irish Club.
Joined the French Army with the intention of bringing help from France to
Ireland. Sailed with a French fleet to Lough Swilly where he was captured.
Court martialled in Dublin, he was sentenced to be hanged, but took his
own life in prison.*

To a Shade

If you have revisited the town, thin Shade,
Whether to look upon your monument
(I wonder if the builder has been paid)
Or happier-thoughted when the day is spent
To drink of that salt breath out of the sea
When grey gulls flit about instead of men,
And the gaunt houses put on majesty:
Let these content you and be gone again;
For they are at their old tricks yet.
                              A man
Of your own passionate serving kind who had brought
In his full hands what, had they only known,
Had given their children's children loftier thought,
Sweeter emotion, working in their veins
Like gentle blood, has been driven from the place,
And insult heaped upon him for his pains,
And for his open-handedness, disgrace;
Your enemy, an old foul mouth, had set
The pack upon him.
                    Go, unquiet wanderer,
And gather the Glasnevin coverlet
About your head till the dust stops your ear,
The time for you to taste of that salt breath
And listen at the corners has not come;
You had enough of sorrow before death —
Away, away! You are safer in the tomb.

September 29, 1913

66

The 'Shade' or ghost is that of Charles Stewart Parnell, leader of the Irish Parliamentary Party who was deposed on the disclosure of his affair with Mrs Kitty O'Shea. 'A man' refers to Hugh Lane, Lady Gregory's nephew whose offer of a gift of French Impressionist paintings to Dublin was repudiated by Dublin Corporation. He died on the Lusitania*. William Martin Murphy, the 'old foul mouth' of the poem, was proprietor of two popular Dublin newspapers and organiser of the great Lockout of 1913, against which Yeats protested publicly.*

An Irish Airman Foresees his Death

I know that I shall meet my fate
Somewhere among the clouds above;
Those that I fight I do not hate,
Those that I guard I do not love;
My country is Kiltartan Cross,
My countrymen Kiltartan's poor,
No likely end could bring them loss
Or leave them happier than before.
Nor law, nor duty bade me fight,
Nor public men, nor cheering crowds,
A lonely impulse of delight
Drove to this tumult in the clouds;
I balanced all, brought all to mind,
The years to come seemed waste of breath,
A waste of breath the years behind
In balance with this life, this death.

This poem is for Robert Gregory, only child of Lady Gregory,
who was killed in action on the Italian Front in 1918.

Easter 1916

I have met them at close of day
Coming with vivid faces
From counter or desk among grey
Eighteenth-century houses.
I have passed with a nod of the head
Or polite meaningless words,
Or have lingered awhile and said
Polite meaningless words,
And thought before I had done
Of a mocking tale or a gibe
To please a companion
Around the fire at the club,
Being certain that they and I
But lived where motley is worn:
All changed, changed utterly:
A terrible beauty is born.

That woman's days were spent
In ignorant good-will,
Her nights in argument
Until her voice grew shrill.
What voice more sweet than hers
When, young and beautiful,
She rode to harriers?
This man had kept a school
And rode our wingèd horse;
This other his helper and friend
Was coming into his force;
He might have won fame in the end,
So sensitive his nature seemed,
So daring and sweet his thought.
This other man I had dreamed
A drunken, vainglorious lout.
He had done most bitter wrong
To some who are near my heart,
Yet I number him in the song;
He, too, has resigned his part
In the casual comedy;
He, too, has been changed in his turn,
Transformed utterly:
A terrible beauty is born.

Hearts with one purpose alone
Through summer and winter seem
Enchanted to a stone
To trouble the living stream.
The horse that comes from the road,
The rider, the birds that range
From cloud to tumbling cloud,
Minute by minute they change;
A shadow of cloud on the stream
Changes minute by minute;
A horse-hoof slides on the brim,
And a horse plashes within it;
The long-legged moor-hens dive,
And hens to moor-cocks call;
Minute by minute they live:
The stone's in the midst of all.

Too long a sacrifice
Can make a stone of the heart.
O when may it suffice?
That is Heaven's part, our part
To murmur name upon name,
As a mother names her child
When sleep at last has come
On limbs that had run wild.
What is it but nightfall?
No, no, not night but death;
Was it needless death after all?
For England may keep faith
For all that is done and said.
We know their dream; enough
To know they dreamed and are dead;
And what if excess of love
Bewildered them till they died?
I write it out in a verse —
MacDonagh and MacBride
And Connolly and Pearse
Now and in time to be,
Wherever green is worn,
Are changed, changed utterly:
A terrible beauty is born.

September 25, 1916

In Easter week 1916, a small group of Irish Volunteers occupied the GPO and other centres in Dublin and held out against British troops until eventually forced to surrender. Fifteen of the leaders were executed by firing squad, making them into national heroes. The man who 'kept school' is Padraig Pearse; Thomas MacDonagh, a poet and dramatist, is Pearse's 'helper and friend'. Even Major John MacBride, who, having married Maud Gonne, the love of Yeats's life, had 'done most bitter wrong' is credited as having 'resigned his part'. The woman who 'rode to harriers' is Countess Markievicz. Connolly is James Connolly, a socialist and trade union leader, who was wounded in the Rising and executed while tied to a chair.

Sixteen Dead Men

O but we talked at large before
The sixteen men were shot,
But who can talk of give and take,
What should be and what not
While those dead men are loitering there
To stir the boiling pot?

You say that we should still the land
Till Germany's overcome;
But who is there to argue that
Now Pearse is deaf and dumb?
And is their logic to outweigh
MacDonagh's bony thumb?

How could you dream they'd listen
That have an ear alone
For those new comrades they have found,
Lord Edward and Wolfe Tone,
Or meddle with our give and take
That converse bone to bone?

The sixteen dead men are the fifteen executed leaders of the 1916 Rising, and Roger Casement, who was hanged in August 1916.

The Rose Tree

'O words are lightly spoken,'
Said Pearse to Connolly,
'Maybe a breath of politic words
Has withered our Rose Tree;
Or maybe but a wind that blows
Across the bitter sea.'

'It needs to be but watered,'
James Connolly replied,
'To make the green come out again
And spread on every side,
And shake the blossom from the bud
To be the garden's pride.'

'But where can we draw water,'
Said Pearse to Connolly,
'When all the wells are parched away?
O plain as plain can be
There's nothing but our own red blood
Can make a right Rose Tree.'

In Memory of Eva Gore-Booth
and Con Markiewicz

The light of evening, Lissadell,
Great windows open to the south,
Two girls in silk kimonos, both
Beautiful, one a gazelle.
But a raving autumn shears
Blossom from the summer's wreath;
The older is condemned to death,
Pardoned, drags out lonely years
Conspiring among the ignorant.
I know now what the younger dreams —
Some vague Utopia — and she seems,
When withered old and skeleton-gaunt,
An image of such politics.
Many a time I think to seek
One or the other out and speak
Of that old Georgian mansion, mix
Pictures of the mind, recall
That table and the talk of youth,
Two girls in silk kimonos, both
Beautiful, one a gazelle.

Dear shadows, now you know it all,
All the folly of a fight
With a common wrong or right.
The innocent and the beautiful
Have no enemy but time;
Arise and bid me strike a match
And strike another till time catch;
Should the conflagration climb,
We the great gazebo built,
Run till all the sages know,
They convicted us of guilt;
Bid me strike a match and blow.

October 1927

OLD AGE AND DEATH

Sailing to Byzantium

I

That is no country for old men. The young
In one another's arms, birds in the trees
- Those dying generations — at their song,
The salmon-falls, the mackerel-crowded seas,
Fish, flesh, or fowl, commend all summer long
Whatever is begotten, born, and dies.
Caught in that sensual music all neglect
Monuments of unageing intellect.

II

An aged man is but a paltry thing,
A tattered coat upon a stick, unless
Soul clap its hands and sing, and louder sing
For every tatter in its mortal dress,
Nor is there singing school but studying
Monuments of its own magnificence;
And therefore I have sailed the seas and come
To the holy city of Byzantium.

III

O sages standing in God's holy fire
As in the gold mosaic of a wall,
Come from the holy fire, perne in a gyre,
And be the singing-masters of my soul.
Consume my heart away; sick with desire
And fastened to a dying animal
It knows not what it is; and gather me
Into the artifice of eternity.

IV

Once out of nature I shall never take
My bodily form from any natural thing,
But such a form as Grecian goldsmiths make
Of hammered gold and gold enamelling
To keep a drowsy Emperor awake;
Or set upon a golden bough to sing
To lords and ladies of Byzantium
Of what is past, or passing, or to come.

1927

The Wheel

Through winter-time we call on spring,
And through the spring on summer call,
And when abounding hedges ring
Declare that winter's best of all;
And after that there's nothing good
Because the spring-time has not come —
Nor know that what disturbs our blood
Is but its longing for the tomb.

Youth and Age

Much did I rage when young,
Being by the world oppressed,
But now with flattering tongue
It speeds the parting guest.

1924

What Then?

His chosen comrades thought at school
He must grow a famous man;
He thought the same and lived by rule,
All his twenties crammed with toil;
'What then?' sang Plato's ghost. 'What then?'

Everything he wrote was read,
After certain years he won
Sufficient money for his need,
Friends that have been friends indeed;
'What then?' sang Plato's ghost. 'What then?'

All his happer dreams came true —
A small house, wife, daughter, son,
Grounds where plum and cabbage grew,
Poets and Wits about him drew;
'What then?' sang Plato's ghost. 'What then?'

'The work I s done', grown old he thought,
'According to my boyish plan;
Let the fools rage, I swerved in nought,
Something to perfection brought';
'What then?' sang Plato's ghost. 'What then?'

Under Ben Bulben

VI

Under bare Ben Bulben's head
In Drumcliff churchyard Yeats is laid.
An ancestor was rector there
Long years ago, a church stands near,
By the road an ancient cross.
No marble, no conventional phrase;
On limestone quarried near the spot
By his command these words are cut:

> Cast a cold eye
> On life, on death.
> Horseman, pass by!

September 4, 1938

The last three lines of the poem are carved as an epitaph on Yeats's tombstone in Drumcliffe churchyard under Ben Bulben.

Cast a cold Eye

On Life, on Death.

Horseman, pass by!

W B YEATS

June 13th 1865

January 28th 1939

WILLIAM BUTLER YEATS
1 8 6 5 - 1 9 3 9
BIOGRAPHICAL SUMMARY

1865 Born in Sandymount, Dublin, the son of John Butler Yeats and Susan (*née* Pollexfen) both of Sligo.

1867 The family moves to London and makes frequent visits to Sligo, spending the summers with his Pollexfen grandparents. The Yeats parents have another son, Jack, and later, two daughters, Elizabeth and Susan, known respectively as Lolly and Lily.

1881 The family moves to Howth, County Dublin. WB Yeats attends The High School, Harcourt Street, Dublin until 1883.

1884 Enrolls at Metropolitan School of Art, Dublin.

1885 Meets John O'Leary, the old Fenian who helped to shape his interest in national politics. Publishes his first poems.

1887 Family moves to London again and Yeats moves into London's literary circles; meets Oscar Wilde, G B Shaw and William Morris.

1889 Yeats meets Maud Gonne in London and falls in love with her; his love for her was to dominate his life and work for the next thirty years during which time he proposed marriage to her many times.

1894 Meets Constance and Eva Gore-Booth at their home in Lissadell, in Sligo.

1896 Meets Lady Gregory of Coole Park, an estate near Gort in south

County Galway. From 1897 spends the first of many summers at Coole. Part of a circle of literary people of which Lady Gregory was the centre. Meets J M Synge, the Irish playwright in Paris and urges him to go to the Aran Islands.

1899 Yeat's play *The Countess Cathleen* performed in Dublin. *The Wind Among the Reeds* published. Yeats active in establishing literary societies in Dublin and London.

1903 Yeat's first American lecture tour. Maud Gonne marries Major John MacBride.

1904 The Abbey Theatre opens in Dublin with Yeats as producer-manager. His play *On Baile's Strand* performed there in December. Became a Director of the theatre in the following year.

1908 Yeat's *Collected Works* published.

1911 Meets Georgina Hyde-Lees who was to become his future wife.

1912 Hugh Lane gift of modern paintings rejected by Dublin Corporation to the disgust of Yeats who was to campaign for many years for their return to Dublin.

1913 Yeats supports the workers in the great Dublin Lock-out.

1916 The Easter Rising in Dublin followed by the executions of sixteen men, including John MacBride, calls forth Yeats's responses in poetry. Yeats again proposes to Maud Gonne, is refused and in the following year proposes to her daughter Iseult who also refuses him.

1917 Buys a ruined tower-house, Thoor Ballylee near Coole Park. Marries Georgina Hyde-Lees and together they set about restoring the tower as a summer home.

1919 His daughter, Anne Butler Yeats born.

1921 His son, William Michael Yeats, born. *Michael Robartes and the Dancer* published. Yeats supports the Anglo-Irish Treaty in the Civil War.

1922 *The Trembling of the Veil* published. Yeats a senator in the new Irish Free State. Major contributions to debates. Speaks in favour of divorce in 1925 and against the censorship of books in 1928.

1923 Awarded the Nobel Prize for Literature.

1926 *A Vision* published.

1928 *The Tower* published. Suffering from ill-health and begins wintering in southern Europe. His last Senate speech in July of that year.

1932 Lady Gregory dies. Yeats leases Riversdale, a country house at Rathfarnham, County Dublin.

1933 *The Winding Stair and Other Poems* published.

1938 His last public appearance at the Abbey Theatre in August. Maud Gonne visits him for the last time at Riversdale. In October, Yeats goes to the South of France in the hope of improving his health.

1939 Dies in France, 28 January. Buried at Roquebrune. In 1948, in fulfilment of his wish, his remains brought to Ireland for his burial in Drumcliffe churchyard, Sligo

DESIGNER'S NOTE

WB Yeats revered the book, as an object as much as a vehicle of information. He believed that the cover of a book and its visual content could be made to work on the imagination of the reader and draw them further into the poetry. To this end it was important to him to collaborate with artists in order to achieve his vision of a book of poetry.

Two artists in particular stand out on his publications: Althea Gyles and Thomas Sturge Moore. Gyles's covers for *The Secret Rose*, *The Wind Among the Reeds* and *The Shadowy Waters*, and Thomas Sturge Moore's covers for *Responsibilities*, *Per Amica Silentia Lunea*, *The Wild Swans at Coole* and *The Winding Stair* use symbols to represent the many sources from which they draw, ie nature, Celtic Art and The Hermetic Order of the Golden Dawn. The five chapter dividers and the cover that I have created for *Best-Loved Yeats* take their inspiration from the mesmerising covers of Gyles and Moore and the poetry that, in turn, inspired them.

Whilst each drawing is different, there are certain structures that appear throughout. They all utilise Golden Section or Golden Ratio to divide the page. This is a geometric system of division that was used throughout history, especially in, but not limited to medieval manuscripts, such as The Book of Kells.

The image works in a central panel, and then there are separate images in the left and right hand panels, usually repeated seven times, as seven is an important astronomical number.

The Enchanted Land

Yeats was obsessed with Celtic folklore. Images of the Fairy, 'The Stolen Child' and 'A Faery Song', combine with a roadway that leads to Knocknarea, the alleged tomb of Queen Maeve. There are also representations of the fruit of the hazel tree on the left and apple blossom on the right, as both of these trees are used metaphorically in poems such as 'The Song of Wandering Aengus' along with the sun and the moon

The silver apples of the moon,
The golden apples of the sun.

The Romantic Idealist

The poems of this period show the influence of Maud Gonne. The main icon is of the highly stylised rose, an image of love, used by The Hermetic Order of the Golden Dawn. The seagull at the top of the drawing is a metaphor for Maud Gonne from the poem 'The White Birds', whilst at the bottom there is a running mountain hare from the poem 'Memory', which could be a symbol for Yeats himself. The two other highly stylised images are of fire and water, opposing elements, a metaphor for the relationship between Yeats and Maud Gonne.

Coole Park and Thoor Ballylee

Coole Park was the home of Lady Gregory, an important figure in Irish cultural life. The swan at the centre is a reference to the poem 'The Wild Swans at Coole', an important period where Yeats's love for Maud Gonne died. The leaves in the left panel are a reference to the Seven Woods at Coole, whilst on the right there is a representation of the stars of the Plaeides or the Seven Sisters. The tower-house in the centre is Thoor Ballylee, home to Yeats and his wife George Hyde Lees, whom he married in 1917. As they were both interested in the occult, there is a moon in a circular sun atop the castle. The lyre in the bottom left represents Apollo, the great archer. This and the image of the Pigeon are referred to in 'In the Seven Woods'.

War and Politics

Yeats was heavily involved in the politics of Ireland, particularly the aftermath of the 1916 Easter Rising, and it hugely influenced his poetry. The symbols here show Pegasus the flying horse as referred to in 'Easter 1916', a metaphor for Padraig Pearse; above this icon there are some flying geese, a visual reference to the Wild Geese from the poem 'September 1913'. The panel to the right has arum lilies, a nationalist symbol. To the left there is a rose tree from 'The Rose Tree' and to the front a drawing of Lissadell House with a gazelle in the front – a reference to Eva Goore-Booth from 'In Memory of Eva Gore-Booth and Con Markiewicz'.

Old Age and Death

The large symbol in the centre of this is based on the icon of The Hermetic Order of the Golden Dawn, the occult organisation of which Yeats was a member. Below it are several classical references: Plato's ghost from 'What Then?' which looks down on and presides over the Hagia Sophia, one of the earliest Christian Churches in Byzantium, present day Istanbul. The panel to the right shows Grecian urns as a symbol of classical art from 'Sailing to Byzantium':

But such a form as Grecian goldsmiths make

Of hammered gold and gold enamelling

The panel to the left shows The Winding Stair, echoing Thomas Sturge Moore's design for the volume of the same name written at this period.

Emma Byrne

January 2010

Index of First Lines